OVERLOOKED MILESTONES OF BLACK HISTORY

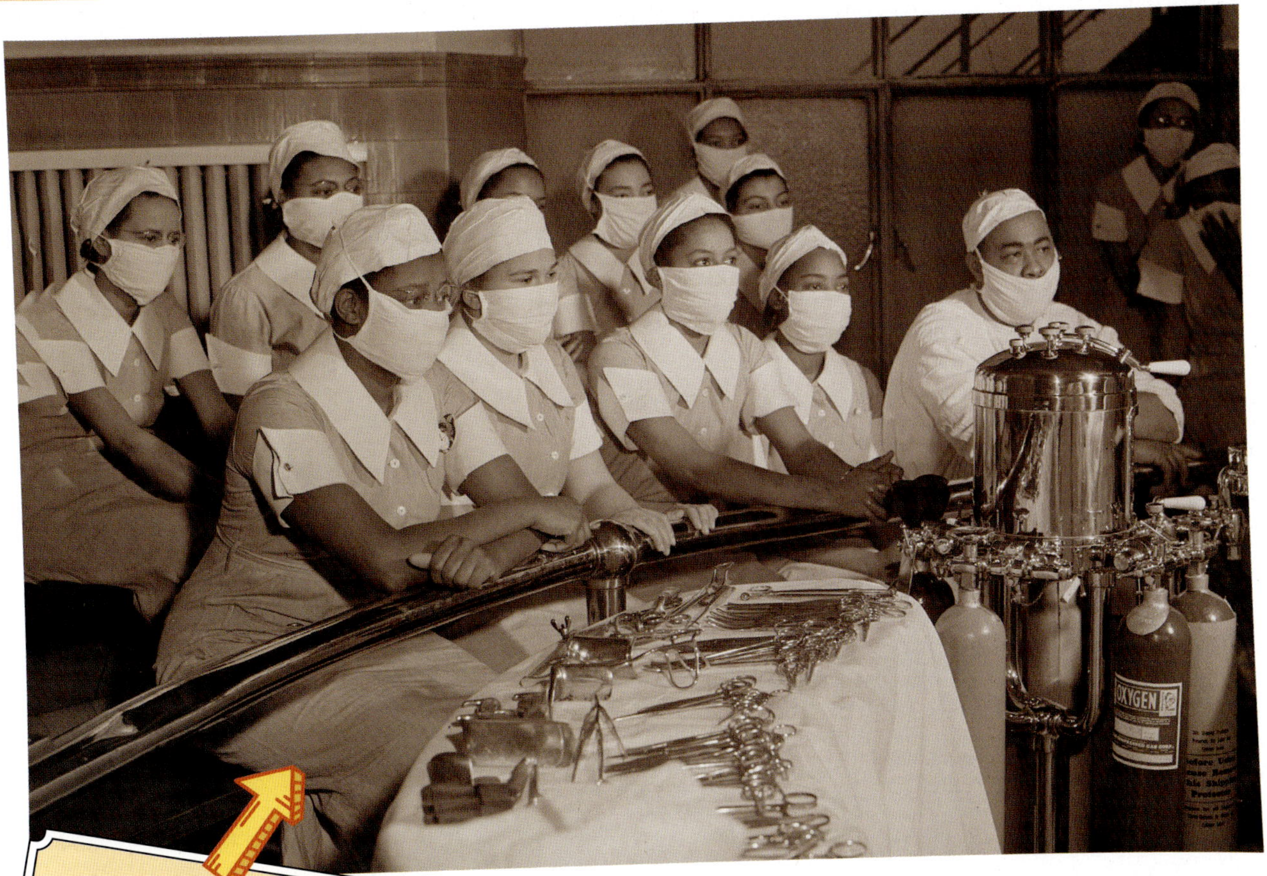

Why is this group of nurses important? Turn to page 27 to discover the answer.

BY KAAVONIA HINTON

Children's Press®
An imprint of Scholastic Inc.

Special thanks to our content consultant and sensitivity reader Deirdre Lynn Hollman, Senior Curriculum Specialist from the Black Education Research Center at Teachers College, Columbia University.

Library of Congress Cataloging-in-Publication Data available
978-1-5461-7802-6 (library binding) | 978-1-5461-7803-3 (paperback) | 978-1-5461-7813-2 (ebook)

10 9 8 7 6 5 4 3 2 1 26 27 28 29 30

Printed in China 62
First edition, 2026

Book design by Kathleen Petelinsek
Series produced by Spooky Cheetah Press

TABLE OF CONTENTS

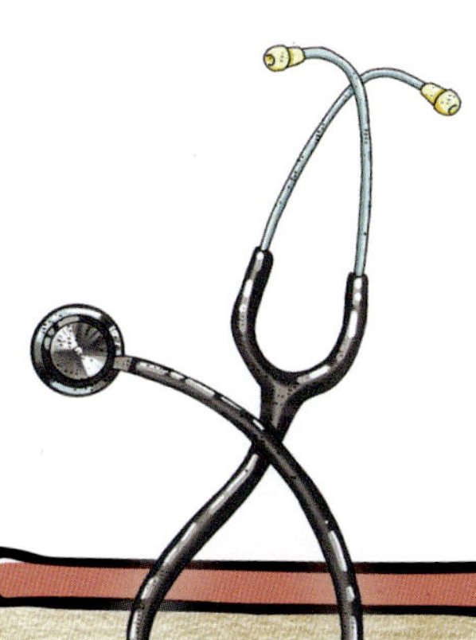

INTRODUCTION

When you think about important events in Black history, what comes to mind? You might think of the 1954 US Supreme Court ruling that declared **school segregation** illegal. Maybe the **integration** of William Frantz Elementary School in New Orleans, Louisiana, comes to mind. On November 14, 1960, six-year-old **Ruby Bridges** became the school's first—and only—Black student.

But there are probably many other important events in Black history that might be unknown to you—lesser-known moments that have also shaped the history of the United States. This book shines a spotlight on ten such moments. These ten "overlooked milestones" include incredible medical advances, daring military strikes, trailblazing protests, and more!

Celebrating the end of school segregation

Officers had to protect Ruby Bridges at school.

Learning about these events deepens our understanding of how Black Americans shaped the country we live in today. Celebrating these milestones encourages us to value them. It allows us to expand our understanding of American history.

Turn the page to discover the powerful stories behind these important events.

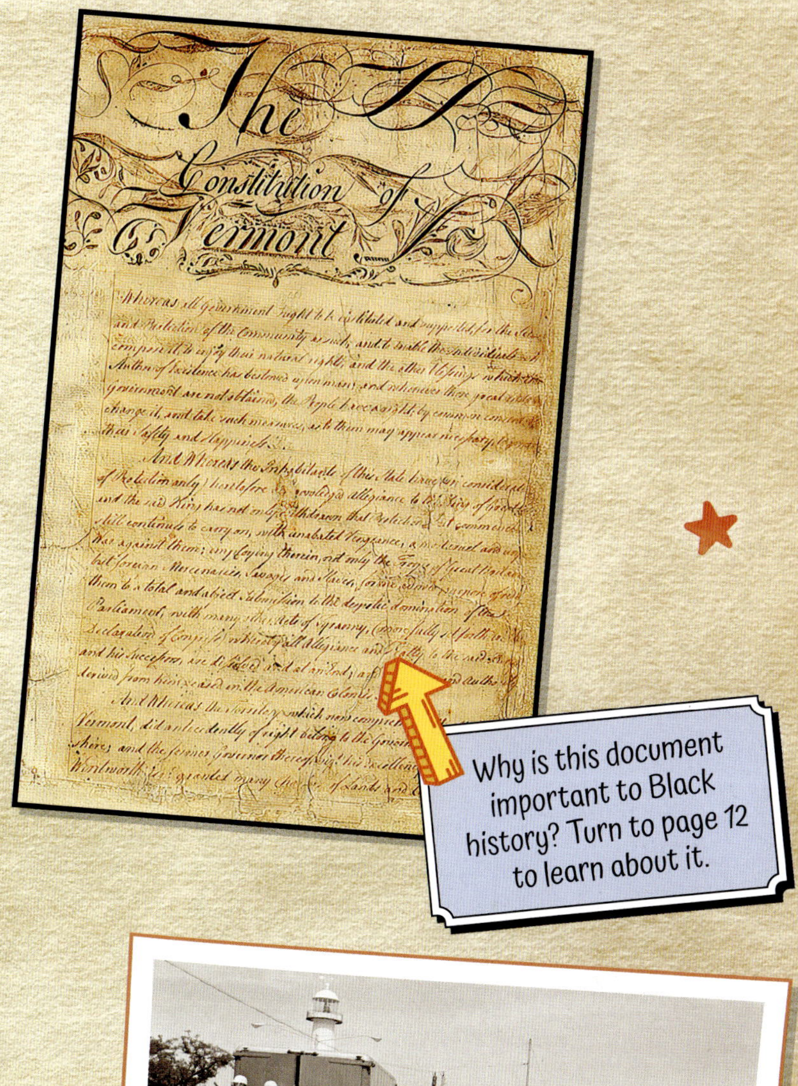
The Constitution of Vermont

Why is this document important to Black history? Turn to page 12 to learn about it.

Who is this woman? Turn to page 21 to learn the answer.

Why is this car upside down? Turn to page 32 to find out.

FIRST DOCUMENTED PERSON BORN INTO SLAVERY

c. 1624

It is impossible to know how William Tucker's parents felt when William was **baptized** in 1624. Antoney and Isabella had no choice about it. In fact, they had no control over any part of their lives. Antoney and Isabella were **enslaved**—and so was their son.

Antoney and Isabella were two of the first enslaved Africans brought to the British colonies in North America. They arrived in 1619 with about twenty other enslaved men and women. Their **son William** was the first documented person to be born into **slavery** in the British colonies in North America. For many, his birth marks the beginning of African American identity in what would become the United States.

Uncovered!

Baby William and his family are listed as Captain William Tucker's property in the 1624–1625 **census**. It was the first detailed census ever taken in British North America.

What Is Slavery?

For nearly two hundred years, about five hundred thousand Black people from Africa were kidnapped, brought to what would become the United States, and sold to enslavers. Enslaved people had no freedom. They suffered physical abuse and were forced to work for no pay—which made many enslavers rich. This was the first time in history that people were enslaved for life based only on their race.

MARYLAND BANS INTERRACIAL MARRIAGE

September 20, 1664

Many people dream of marrying the love of their life. For a long time that was an impossible dream for a lot of people in America. In 1664, Maryland became the first colony to make marriage between a Black person and a white person against the law. Over time, other colonies passed similar laws.

One reason these laws were passed was to justify the continuation of slavery. Enslavers argued that Black people were different from white people. They worried that if a Black person married a white person, it would be admitting that there was no real difference between the races. It took hundreds of years of legal battles before bans on interracial marriage were ruled **unconstitutional**.

Uncovered!

In 2000, Alabama became the last US state to **abolish** its law banning interracial marriage.

Spreading the Love

Nine states never had laws against interracial marriage, but many others did. Over the years, some states got rid of the ban. But by 1967, those laws still existed in sixteen states. That year, a case called *Loving v. Virginia* went to the US Supreme Court. The court ruled that the ban on interracial marriage was unconstitutional.

Mildred and Richard Loving

THE STONO REBELLION

September 9, 1739

By 1739, more than one hundred thousand people were enslaved in the British colonies in North America. They lived under horrific conditions. Enslaved people used many strategies to try to gain freedom. Rebellion was one of them.

SOUTH CAROLINA

Stono River

GEORGIA

Fort Mose

FLORIDA

The largest rebellion in the colonies took place in South Carolina on September 9, 1739. That day, twenty enslaved people left the plantations where they lived and worked and met near the **Stono River**. The group was led by an enslaved man named Jemmy. The group killed two people working at a shop and took weapons from the store.

The rebels then headed south toward **Fort Mose** in present-day Florida. At the time, Florida was a Spanish territory. Just one year earlier, Spanish leaders had declared that enslaved people who reached the fort would be free.

More than sixty other enslaved people joined the group as they traveled south. They fought and killed about twenty-five white people before clashing with a group of enslavers and **militiamen**.

Today, Fort Mose is a national historic site.

Uncovered!

The Stono Rebellion was the largest and most violent **insurrection** in the British colonies before the American Revolution.

A Bitter Struggle

The freedom seekers refused to surrender, and a **fight started** between the two sides. In the end, however, the resistance was put down. A few of the rebels were able to escape. Many were killed during the fighting. Others were arrested and then put to death.

10 48

THE STONO REBELLION (1739)

The Stono Rebellion, the largest slave insurrection in British North America, began nearby on September 9, 1739. About 20 Africans raided a store near Wallace Creek, a branch of the Stono River. Taking guns and other weapons, they killed two shopkeepers. The rebels marched south toward promised freedom in Spanish Florida, waving flags, beating drums, and shouting "Liberty!"

(Continued on other side)

This sign celebrating the Stono Rebellion is in Rantowles, South Carolina.

Although the Stono Rebellion failed, it terrified many white people. There were already several harsh laws to control enslaved people. After the rebellion, those laws were strengthened. Still, enslaved people continued to find ways to resist.

Making It Difficult to Seek Freedom

After the Stono Rebellion, South Carolina passed the Negro Act of 1740. The law was meant to prevent future rebellions. Among other restrictions, enslaved people were not allowed to meet in groups. They were not allowed to learn to read or write. They could not even play a drum or horn, because instruments could be used to communicate plans for an escape or uprising.

"AFRICAN SLAVERY IN AMERICA" IS PUBLISHED

March 8, 1775

The American Revolution began in 1775. American leaders said they were fighting for liberty. Yet the practice of slavery existed throughout the colonies. And enslaved people were not free. Many people thought slavery was unfair and wanted it to end. They were called **abolitionists**. Abolitionists argued against slavery in speeches and in writing. They thought the new country should live up to its ideals.

An abolitionist meeting in Boston, Massachusetts

On March 8, 1775, one of the first arguments for abolishing slavery was published. It was an essay titled **"African Slavery in America."** The essay appeared in a newspaper called *The Pennsylvania Journal and Weekly Advertiser*. It was written in the form of a letter to America. It was signed from "Justice and Humanity." The essay said enslaved people had a natural right to be free. It also pointed out the colonists' **hypocrisy** in fighting for their own liberty while enslaving other people.

I.

AFRICAN SLAVERY IN AMERICA.

Messrs. BRADFORD,
Please to insert the following, and oblige yours A. B.

TO AMERICANS.

THAT some desperate wretches should be willing to steal and enslave men by violence and murder for gain, is rather lamentable than strange. But that many civilized, nay, christianized people should approve, and be concerned in the savage practice, is surprising; and still persist, though it has been so often proved contrary to the light of nature, to every principle of Justice and Humanity, and even good policy, by a succession of eminent men,* and several late publications.

Our Traders in MEN (*an unnatural commodity!*) must know the wickedness of that SLAVE-TRADE, if they attend to reasoning, or the dictates of their own hearts; and such as shun and stiffle all these, wilfully sacrifice Conscience, and the character of integrity to that golden Idol.

The Managers of that Trade themselves, and others, testify, that many of these African nations inhabit fertile

* Dr. Ames, Baxter, Durham, Locke, Carmichael, Hutcheson, Montesquieu, and Blackstone, Wallace, etc., etc. Bishop of Gloucester.—*Author.*

[What work of Dr. (? William) Ames is referred to I have not found. The others are Baxter's "Christian Directory"; James Durham's "Law Unsealed"; John Locke's "Of Government"; Gerschomus Carmichael's "Puffendorf"; Francis Hutcheson's "System of Moral Philosophy"; Montesquieu's "Spirit of the Laws"; Blackstone's "Commentaries"; Dr. George Wallace on the ancient peerages of Scotland; "Sermon before the Society for the Propagation of the Gospel, 21 February 1766," by the Bishop of Gloucester (Warburton). —*Editor.*]

4

Who Wrote It?

We do not know who wrote the essay. The author did not sign his or her real name. Some people think **Thomas Paine** was the author. In 1776, Paine published a pamphlet titled *Common Sense*, which said colonists should fight for their independence. Paine did not write much about slavery, though. That is why others believe it is unlikely that Paine wrote "African Slavery in America." Even if the author of the essay is still a mystery, its effect on people is not. A few weeks after "African Slavery in America" was published, the first **antislavery society** in the United States was formed in Philadelphia, Pennsylvania.

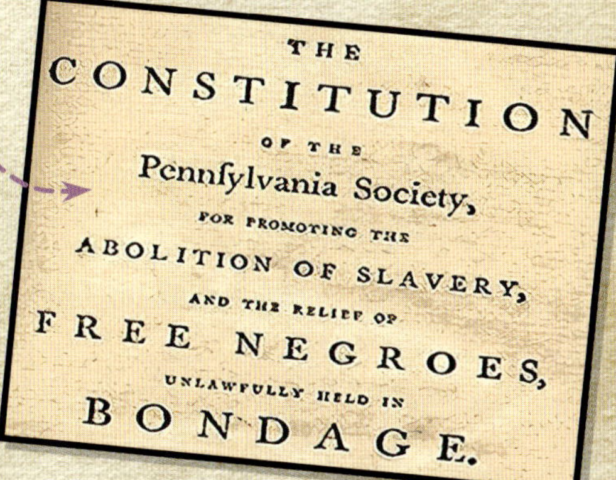

THE CONSTITUTION OF THE Pennfylvania Society, FOR PROMOTING THE ABOLITION OF SLAVERY, AND THE RELIEF OF FREE NEGROES, UNLAWFULLY HELD IN BONDAGE.

Constitutional Compromise

In 1787, **delegates** from twelve of the thirteen US states met in Philadelphia, Pennsylvania, to draft the US Constitution. Among the issues they debated was whether slavery should continue or be abolished. Many delegates were enslavers themselves. Some of the enslavers, including George Washington and Thomas Jefferson, thought slavery should end eventually. But they did not wish to risk their own financial security immediately. The leaders made compromises when writing the Constitution. One of those stated that the importation of enslaved people from Africa would end within twenty years.

Uncovered!

The words *slave* and *slavery* do not appear in the US Constitution. The drafters did not want this institution to be mentioned in a document that they hoped would last forever.

VERMONT STARTS TO BAN SLAVERY

July 2, 1777

In 1777, war was raging in America. The colonists were fighting for independence from Great Britain. Things were clearly changing in the colonies. That was especially true in Vermont, which had originally been part of the colony of New York.

In July, Vermont declared itself independent of Great Britain—and of the colony of New York. As an independent nation, Vermont quickly adopted a **written constitution**. It was the first in North America to partially ban slavery.

This building was where Vermont's first constitution was signed. At the time, it was a tavern.

Uncovered!
Vermont did not become part of the United States until 1791. That is when it became the fourteenth state.

Limited Freedom

Vermont's constitution made it illegal to enslave any male over the age of twenty-one or any female over the age of eighteen. However, children who were already enslaved remained so until they reached the required age.

It is believed that Dinah Mattis was the first enslaved person freed in Vermont.

Once adult enslaved people were freed, their liberty remained limited in many ways. Free Black people in Vermont also experienced **racism** and segregation. Segregation was the practice of separating Black and white people and having different rules for each group. It denied Black people quality jobs, housing, and education for many years.

Clotilda

In 1808, the US government made it illegal to bring enslaved people into the country from Africa. However, people continued to do so illegally. In 1860, the cargo ship *Clotilda* docked in Alabama. More than one hundred enslaved African women, men, and children were on board. It was the last documented ship to bring enslaved Africans to the United States.

The *Clotilda* was a schooner, like this ship.

THE DENMARK VESEY CONSPIRACY IS DISCOVERED

1822

Denmark Vesey was born around 1767 and was enslaved as a child. He was living in Charleston, South Carolina, in 1799 when he won $1,500 in a lottery. Vesey purchased his freedom for $600 one month later. He used the rest of the money to start a carpentry business. Vesey did not have enough money to buy his children's freedom, though. He knew that his children's enslavers could sell them at any time—and that he would not know how to find them. That might have motivated Vesey to organize one of the largest insurrections in the United States.

Self-Purchase

Vesey was not the only enslaved person able to buy his freedom. Some people earned small amounts of money by **selling vegetables** or working as tradespeople. After years of saving, some managed to purchase their freedom. However, this was rare. Most enslavers did not permit it.

Plotting the Insurrection

Laws in South Carolina said anyone involved in an insurrection—enslaved or free—would be killed. Yet Vesey did not let that stop him. He joined the African Methodist Episcopal (AME) Church and preached to small groups of enslaved people in his home every week. Vesey used passages from the Bible to convince church members that they had a right to be free. He also read from published abolitionist speeches and essays. By 1822, Vesey and other church leaders had a plan. Freedom seekers would begin killing their enslavers at midnight on Sunday, July 14. Then they would free other enslaved people in the area, rob the city's banks, and escape to Haiti.

The AMC church in Charleston has been rebuilt twice in the years since Denmark Vesey planned his rebellion there.

Uncovered!

Beginning in 1791, enslaved people in Haiti revolted against their French **colonizers**. They won freedom for themselves and, in 1804, gained independence for their island nation.

A Flaw in the Plan

That May, an enslaved man named William Paul asked another enslaved man, Peter Prioleau, to join Vesey's group. Prioleau did not want to join the insurrection. He reported the plot to his enslaver, who then alerted the mayor. Paul was arrested. The next month, another enslaved man named George Wilson learned of the plot. He also told his enslaver. Others involved in the planning were soon arrested, including Vesey.

Almost seventy men were found guilty at trial. Thirty-five of them, including Vesey, were hanged. Some, including white allies, were imprisoned. Others were forced to leave South Carolina.

AN
OFFICIAL REPORT
OF THE
TRIALS OF SUNDRY NEGROES,
CHARGED
WITH AN ATTEMPT TO RAISE
AN INSURRECTION
IN THE STATE OF SOUTH-CAROLINA:
PRECEDED BY AN
INTRODUCTION AND NARRATIVE;
AND
IN AN APPENDIX,
A REPORT OF THE TRIALS OF
FOUR WHITE PERSONS,
ON INDICTMENTS FOR ATTEMPTING TO EXCITE THE SLAVES TO INSURRECTION.
Prepared and Published at the request of the Court.
BY LIONEL H. KENNEDY & THOMAS PARKER,
Members of the Charleston Bar, and the Presiding Magistrates of the Court.
CHARLESTON:
PRINTED BY JAMES R. SCHENCK, 23, BROAD-STREET.
1822.

This is the official report from Denmark Vesey's trial in Charleston, SC.

From the Charleston Mercury, July 3.

The six convicted blacks, who were condemned to death for plotting and at tempting an insurrection in this state, were hanged, yesterday morning, between the hours of six and eight, pursuant to their sentence.

Denmark Vesey—a free black man—Rolla, Batteau, Ned, Peter and Jesse, all five slaves, made up the number.

This is a clipping from the *Philadelphia Inquirer* newspaper.

Backlash

Even though Vesey's plot was discovered and no white people were harmed, the South Carolina government punished the Black community. Because Vesey was a member of the AME church, white people saw it as a threat. They suspected that church meetings were a cover for antislavery activities and destroyed the church building in Charleston. The government also passed the Seaman's Act of 1822. **Free Black sailors** on ships that docked in South Carolina's ports were kept in jail until their ships were ready to leave. Then, in December of that year, a stronghold called the **Citadel** was established to house soldiers. They were there to make sure no other rebellions were hatched in Charleston.

This is a recent photo of the Citadel.

Uncovered!
In 1842, the Citadel became a military college. It still is today.

CLOTEL IS PUBLISHED

December 1853

William Wells Brown is the author of the book *Clotel; or, The President's Daughter*. He was born into enslavement around 1814. When Brown was a teenager, he tried unsuccessfully to escape with his mother. Later, he was separated from his family when his mother, sister, and brothers were sold. Brown escaped from his enslaver on New Year's Day in 1834 and eventually made his way to England. He later wrote his autobiography, *Narrative of William W. Brown, a Fugitive Slave*. That book, and Brown's skill as an antislavery lecturer, made him famous. He was invited to speak about his experiences throughout Europe. Brown was living in London when he published *Clotel* in 1853. It is one of the first novels written by an African American author.

Fugitive Slave Laws

The second Fugitive Slave Act, passed in 1850, required anyone living in a free state to help enslavers recapture freedom seekers who had escaped, like Brown. The law also denied them a jury trial. It was not uncommon for free Black people to be kidnapped and sold into slavery because of the Fugitive Slave Act of 1850.

An Antislavery Novel

Clotel describes the violence and inhumanity of slavery. It tells the story of Currer, a fictional character who is enslaved by **President Thomas Jefferson**, and the daughters they had together—Clotel and Althesa.

Unlike most novels today, the book includes poetry, folk songs, and newspaper articles. It even includes part of Brown's own story, though it is told in the third person. Brown was of mixed race. His mother was Black and his father was white. *Clotel* exposed the abuses Black women and people of mixed race experienced under enslavement. It is also one of the earliest novels that showcases "**passing**." This term describes how some people of mixed race were able to pass as white to escape enslavement. Brown hoped the harsh realities depicted in *Clotel* would convince people to fight against slavery.

President Jefferson enslaved more than six hundred people throughout his lifetime.

Clotel Takes America by Storm

During the winter of 1860–1861, *Clotel* reached readers in the United States. It was published in parts, one week at a time, in a newspaper called ***The Weekly Anglo-African***. A few years later, the story was revised and published as a **book** titled *Clotelle: A Tale of the Southern States* (1864).

The Weekly Anglo-African

VOL. I.—NO. 1. NEW YORK, JULY 23, 1859. PRICE FOUR CENTS.

The Weekly Anglo-African was just one of the abolitionist publications founded by Black journalist Thomas Hamilton.

Brown Was Often First

The story of *Clotel* is fiction, but it was inspired by the real story of Thomas Jefferson and Sally Hemings, a Black woman he enslaved. When Brown wrote *Clotel*, the story that Jefferson fathered Hemings's children was only a rumor. Brown did not have access to the evidence that came out much later to confirm it. But with *Clotel*, Brown was one of the first to fictionalize the real abuse and **exploitation** enslaved women suffered.

In addition to being one of the first Black Americans to publish a novel, Brown is also said to be the first Black American to publish a play, a travel book, and a book about military history.

Thomas Jefferson and Sally Hemings

Beginning in 1802, people published stories in newspapers saying that Thomas Jefferson had children with Sally Hemings. Jefferson did not comment on it. Today, we know Hemings had at least six of Jefferson's children, four of whom survived to adulthood. Some people think their relationship might have been romantic, but this is a controversial issue. Because Hemings was enslaved, she could not say no to any demands made by her enslaver.

THE COMBAHEE RIVER RAID

June 1–2, 1863

By the middle of the 1800s, the United States was divided over the issue of slavery. Some people wanted slavery to spread to new territories. Others, including presidential candidate Abraham Lincoln, did not. Lincoln won the election of 1860. Soon after, in December, South Carolina **seceded** from, or left, the Union. Ultimately, ten other Southern states seceded as well. The first shots of the Civil War between the Union (North) and the Confederacy (South) were fired in 1861.

Black men and women were eager to help the Union win the war. However, they were not officially allowed to join the fighting. That changed in 1863. Some Black men became soldiers. And both men and women helped the Union army in many other ways. They did physical work, such as cooking and cleaning. Some—like **Harriet Tubman**—were scouts and spies. In the summer of 1863, she and Colonel James Montgomery planned and led a **raid** on the Combahee River in South Carolina.

John Brown

John Brown was a white abolitionist. He believed slavery would not end without violence. In 1859, Brown came up with a plan for a raid on the federal **arsenal** at Harpers Ferry, Virginia. Harriet Tubman helped him gather followers. Brown hoped the raid would spark a rebellion and free enslaved people. Brown's mission failed, but the raid pushed the country toward the Civil War.

Spying on the Confederacy

Tubman escaped from enslavement in Maryland in 1849. After that she returned to the South several times to **emancipate** her family and other enslaved people. Tubman was a wanted woman in the region. A reward was offered for her capture. Despite the danger, in 1862, Tubman traveled to South Carolina from her home in Auburn, New York, to work as a spy for the Union army.

By 1860, Harriet Tubman was called the "Moses of her people." In addition to the Combahee raid, she returned to the South thirteen times to lead about seventy people to freedom.

THE MOSES OF HER PEOPLE

AMAZING LIFE WORK OF HARRIET TUBMAN. A STORY STRANGER THAN FICTION. AFTER 80 YEARS OF DEVOTION SHE LIVES TO LAMENT THAT SHE CAN DO NO MORE THAN PLAN.

In the months leading up to the Combahee River raid, Tubman scouted the area in disguise. She pretended to be a field hand—an enslaved person who worked on a plantation. Tubman found out where the Confederates had placed mines to stop Union ships along the river. She learned about the landscape. She even received information from enslaved people about where the Southern troops stored food, weapons, and other supplies.

Uncovered!
Harriet Tubman was the first woman to help lead a raid in the Civil War.

Black Soldiers Lead the Way

On June 1 to 2, 1863, **three Union gunboats sailed up the Combahee River**. Aboard one of those ships were Tubman, Colonel Montgomery, and about one hundred fifty Black soldiers under his command. Tubman was able to guide the boats away from danger and lead the soldiers to where enslaved people were waiting for them. In all, more than seven hundred enslaved people were emancipated. Meanwhile, the Union soldiers went ashore and **destroyed several plantations**.

By the time Confederate troops learned about the raid, they were unable to stop it. The Union caused millions of dollars in damages to the Confederates without losing a single soldier.

The success of the Combahee River raid was reported in the newspapers of major cities, but most of them did not mention Tubman.

Uncovered!
Harriet Tubman was not recognized for her service in the army until 2021.

The Impact of the Raid

The raid gave enslaved people on several plantations their freedom and impacted the war in many ways. About **one hundred of the men who were freed joined the ranks of the Union army**. And removing the enslaved workers from plantations meant there was no one to grow, harvest, and sell planters' crops. That food might have gone to feed Confederate soldiers or to raise money to support the rebellion. Thanks to the work of Harriet Tubman and the Black infantrymen who took part in the Combahee River raid, the Union was one step closer to winning the war.

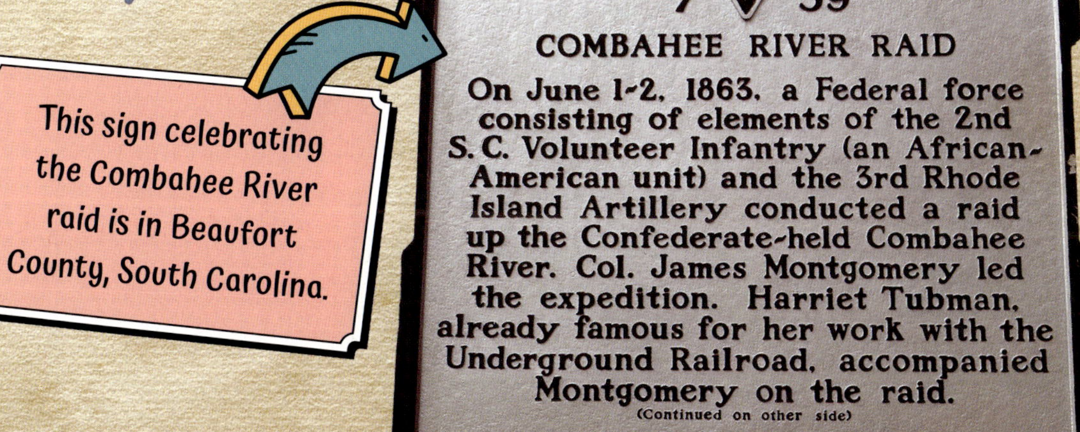

This sign celebrating the Combahee River raid is in Beaufort County, South Carolina.

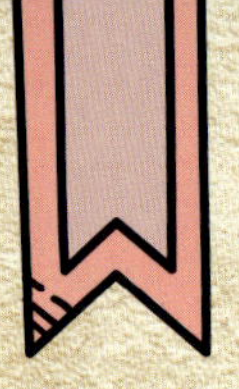

A GROUNDBREAKING SURGERY IS PERFORMED

July 10, 1893

On July 9, 1893, James Cornish was stabbed in the chest during a fight. At the time, hospitals were **segregated**. Because Cornish was Black, he was taken to **Provident Hospital and Training School for Nurses** in Chicago, Illinois. That proved to be a lucky thing. Provident was founded and run by **Dr. Daniel Hale Williams III**. It was the first hospital in America run by a Black person. The next morning, Dr. Williams would save Cornish's life by performing one of the first-ever successful open-heart surgeries.

Reconstruction

Reconstruction was the period after the Civil War devoted to rebuilding the South and securing rights for formerly enslaved people. Three key amendments to the US Constitution were passed during this time. The Thirteenth Amendment ended slavery. The Fourteenth Amendment granted citizenship to Black people. And the Fifteenth Amendment allowed Black men to vote. However, racist policies were often put in place to keep these laws from being enforced. They were known as Jim Crow laws. They included segregation and unfair practices to keep Black people from voting, among other things.

Opening Doors

Daniel Hale Williams III was born free in Pennsylvania in 1856. He studied under a surgeon before completing his training at Chicago Medical College. Because of segregation, Williams was not allowed to work in the existing hospitals in Chicago. He set up his own medical practice and worked to help other Black medical students. With the support of donors like **Frederick Douglass**, Williams opened Provident Hospital and Training School for Nurses on May 4, 1891. It was the country's first hospital and nursing school with an interracial staff.

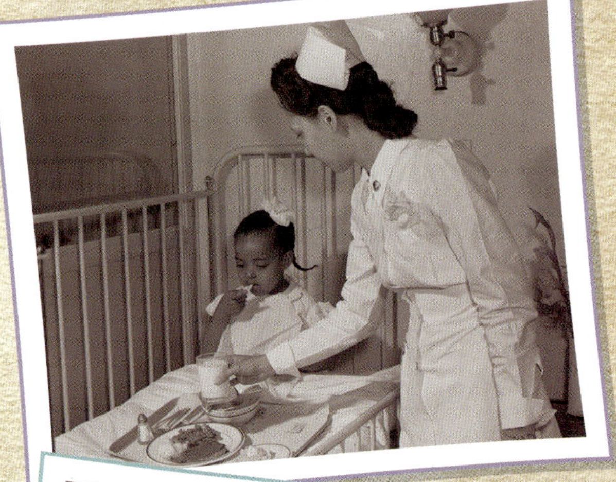

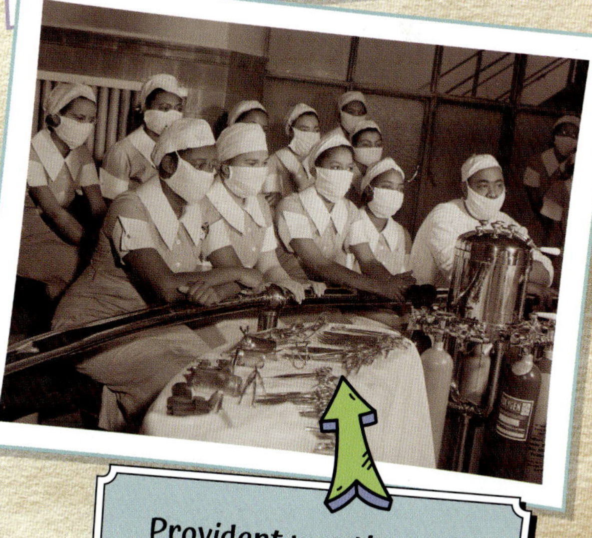

Provident was the first hospital to establish a nursing school to train Black students, like the nurses shown here.

Uncovered!
Former First Lady Michelle Obama was born at Provident Hospital and Training School for Nurses in 1964.

A Lifesaving Decision

When James Cornish was rushed into Williams's hospital, many of the medical methods in use today had not been invented yet. There were no X-rays, so Dr. Williams could not see inside Cornish's chest. Yet he suspected something was wrong with the young man's heart. Williams made the risky decision to operate. At the time it was believed that cutting open a patient's chest would kill them.

A surgical kit from the 1880s

Nevertheless, Williams cut Cornish's chest open. He sewed up the wound in the patient's pericardium, the sac that covers the heart. The surgery was successful. Cornish went on to live a normal life.

Uncovered!

When Dr. Williams started his practice in 1884, he was one of only three Black doctors practicing in Chicago.

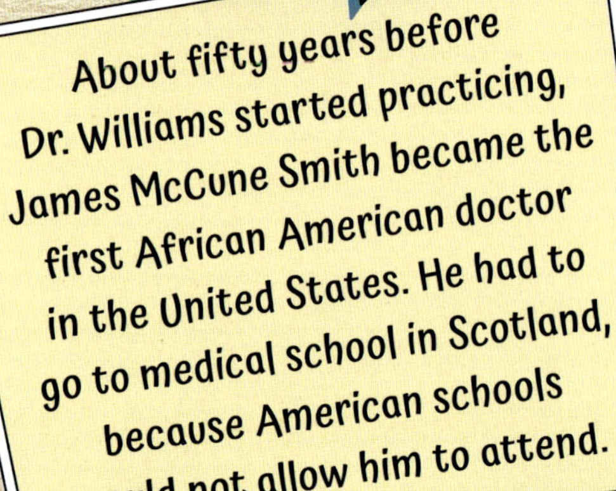

About fifty years before Dr. Williams started practicing, James McCune Smith became the first African American doctor in the United States. He had to go to medical school in Scotland, because American schools would not allow him to attend.

Dr. Williams's Legacy

After performing the successful open-heart surgery on July 10, 1893, Dr. Williams continued to blaze a trail in the medical field. In 1894, he became the chief surgeon at **Freedmen's Hospital** in Washington, DC. It was the highest medical position available to a Black person at the time. Black doctors were not allowed to join the American Medical Association. So Dr. Williams helped found the **National Medical Association for Black doctors**. He was also a founding member of the American College of Surgeons.

Today, thanks to pioneers like Dr. Williams, hospitals and other public facilities in the United States are **integrated**.

THE BILOXI WADE-INS BEGIN

May 14, 1959

In the 1950s, many public facilities were still segregated. For example, in many places, Black people and white people used **separate drinking fountains**, waiting rooms, and schools. Black people were not allowed to use the same public beaches or public pools as white people, either. An important goal of the **Civil Rights Movement** was to strike down these unfair laws and practices.

The first challenge to segregated **beaches in Biloxi, Mississippi**, happened on May 14, 1959. That day, **Dr. Gilbert Mason, Sr.**, tried to go swimming with some friends and their children at Biloxi Beach. A police officer told Mason and his friends they were breaking the law. He ordered them to leave.

Uncovered!
The Biloxi wade-ins were the first major civil rights campaign in Mississippi.

Fighting for Equality

Mason and one of his friends went to the police station to ask if they had broken any laws. But they were not given an answer. They returned to the police station the next day still hoping to get an answer. That is when Mason and his friend were told they would be arrested if they tried to go to the beach again.

Nonviolent protesters like Dr. Mason risked being arrested to fight for their cause.

There were no actual laws banning Black people from the beach, though. White people had routinely enforced segregation in places like beaches even when laws did not require it. Black people were allowed to use only a small section of the beach, and white people were given access to the rest. White people were also allowed to own beachfront property, but Black people were not. Mason decided to do something about these practices.

In 2009, US Route 90 near Biloxi was renamed Dr. Gilbert R. Mason, Sr., Memorial Highway in honor of the fiftieth anniversary of the first wade-in.

CIVIL RIGHTS WADE-INS

On May 14, 1959, April 24, 1960, and June 23, 1963, the Biloxi beach front was the site of planned civil rights wade-ins demanding equal access to the public beach. On April 24, 1960, several citizens, both black and white, were injured and arrested, including the leader of the wade-ins, physician Dr. Gilbert R. Mason Sr. This series of protests gave birth to the Biloxi branch of the NAACP, major voter registration drives in 1960, and a 1968 federal court ruling opening the beach to all citizens.

MISSISSIPPI DEPARTMENT OF ARCHIVES AND HISTORY, 2009

This sign celebrating the wade-ins is at Biloxi Beach.

Bloody Wade-In Day

On April 24, 1960, Mason returned to the beach with more than one hundred twenty protesters, including children. For a while, they swam and played games on the beach. Before long, though, white people attacked the protesters. A few people were shot. Even though Mason was protesting peacefully, he was arrested. Despite this unfair treatment, he and the other protesters were committed to carrying on the fight. Today, April 24, 1960, is known as **Bloody Wade-In Day**.

White people turned over the car of a Black protester during one of the wade-ins.

Black Flag Protest

Protesters carried out another wade-in on May 17, 1960. The final wade-in was held on **June 23, 1963**. It was held in honor of slain civil rights activist **Medgar Evers**. That day, protesters lined the beach carrying black flags. More than two thousand white people attacked the demonstrators. Only the protesters—most of whom were Black—were arrested.

Dr. Gilbert Mason, Sr.

The following year, the 1964 Civil Rights Act officially desegregated Biloxi beaches. However, white people in Biloxi resisted the law. The beaches were not actually integrated until 1968, nearly a decade after the first wade-in.

A Dedicated Activist

Medgar Evers was born on July 2, 1925, in Decatur, Mississippi. He was a World War II **veteran** and an activist who tried unsuccessfully to integrate the University of Mississippi law school. Evers was working for the National Association for the Advancement of Colored People (**NAACP**) when he was murdered on June 12, 1963. Evers was killed by a white supremacist named Byron De La Beckwith.

The NAACP is an organization that was formed in 1909 to fight for equal rights for African Americans.

TIMELINE

You have learned about ten important events that shaped our nation—ten overlooked milestones of Black history. Now you can connect them to some well-known events in Black history. And keep exploring. There are many more overlooked milestones waiting to be celebrated!

c. 1624 The first documented person is born into slavery in the colonies.

September 20, 1664 Maryland bans interracial marriage.

September 9, 1739 The Stono Rebellion takes place.

March 8, 1775 "African Slavery in America" is published.

July 2, 1777 Vermont starts to ban slavery.

1822 The Denmark Vesey conspiracy is discovered.

December 1853 *Clotel* is published.

1600s | 1700s | 1800s

1619 **The first enslaved African people** are brought to the British colonies in North America.

1831 **Nat Turner**, an enslaved Black carpenter and preacher, leads a revolt in Virginia.

1863 The **Emancipation Proclamation** is issued.

1865 The **Thirteenth Amendment** abolishes slavery in the United States.

1896 The US Supreme Court ruling in ***Plessy v. Ferguson*** upholds segregation as long as equal facilities are available.

1947 **Jackie Robinson** signs with the Brooklyn Dodgers, becoming the first Black player in Major League Baseball.

June 1–2, 1863
The Combahee River raid takes place.

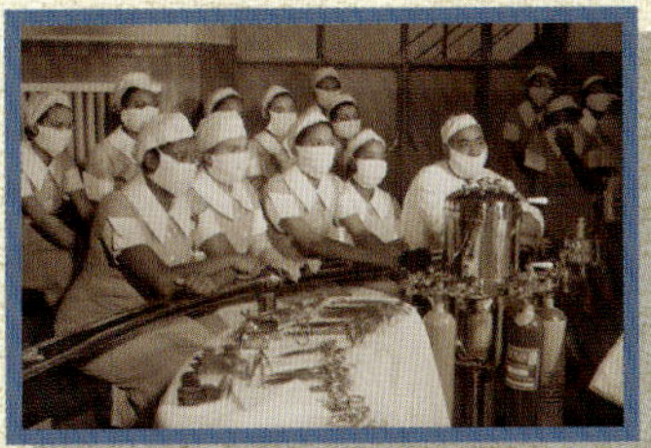

July 10, 1893
One of the first-ever successful open-heart surgeries is performed.

May 14, 1959
The Biloxi wade-ins begin.

The ten overlooked milestones of Black history covered in this book are on the top of the timeline. Well-known events are on the bottom.

1900s **2000s**

1964
The Civil Rights Act is passed.

TODAY
Black Americans continue to fight for their rights and the rights of all citizens of the United States.

1954
The US Supreme Court ruling in ***Brown v. Board of Education of Topeka*** outlaws segregation in schools.

1955
Rosa Parks's arrest sparks the **Montgomery Bus Boycott**, which eventually leads to integration of public transportation.

1960
In February, four students stage a **sit-in** at a segregated lunch counter in **Greensboro, North Carolina**. Similar protests follow across the country, leading to an end of segregation policies in many businesses.

In November, **Ruby Bridges** integrates William Frantz Elementary School in New Orleans.

1963
About 250,000 people take part in the **March on Washington for Jobs and Freedom**.

GLOSSARY

abolish (uh-BAH-lish) to end something officially

abolitionists (ab-uh-LISH-uh-nists) people who worked to end slavery before the Civil War

arsenal (AHR-suh-nuhl) a place where weapons and ammunition are made or stored

baptized (BAP-tized) to have water poured on one's head or be immersed in water, as a sign that one has become a Christian

census (SEN-suhs) an official count of all the people living in a country or district

Civil Rights Movement (SIV-uhl RITES MOOV-muhnt) the fight for racial equality and citizenship in the United States that started in the mid-1950s and became famous for using nonviolent protests and civil disobedience to change unfair laws and practices

colonizers (KAH-luh-nize-urz) nations, kingdoms, or states that forcibly take control of a land and a people other than their own

delegates (DEL-i-gits) people who represent other people at a meeting or in a governing body or group

emancipate (i-MAN-suh-pate) to free from slavery or control

enslaved (en-SLAYVD) held involuntarily and forced to work without pay under threat of violence or death

exploitation (ek-sploy-TAY-shuhn) unfair treatment of someone for the advantage of another

hypocrisy (hi-PAH-kri-see) pretending or claiming to have certain beliefs or feelings but acting in a contradictory manner

insurrection (in-suhr-ECK-shuhn) revolt against a civil authority or an established government

integration (in-tuh-GRAY-shuhn) the act of changing something to include people of all races

militiamen (muh-LISH-uh-men) people who are trained to fight but are not professional soldiers

passing (PAS-ing) when someone acts as if they belong to a racial or ethnic group other than their own based on their skin color and other aspects of their appearance

racism (RAY-si-zuhm) the unfair belief that one race is better than others, leading to mistreatment

raid (RAYD) a sudden, surprise attack on a place

seceded (si-SEE-did) formally withdrew from the United States to form another country

segregation (seg-ri-GAY-shuhn) the practice of separating Black and white people, and having different rules for each group

slavery (SLAY-vur-ee) the practice of holding people as property against their will, forcing them to work for no pay under threat of violence, and denying them the rights held by free persons

unconstitutional (uhn-kahn-sti-TOO-shuh-nuhl) not in keeping with the basic principles or laws set forth in the Constitution of the United States

veteran (VET-ur-uhn) a person who has served in the armed forces, especially during a war

INDEX

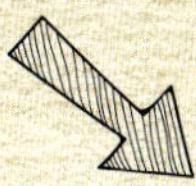

FURTHER READING

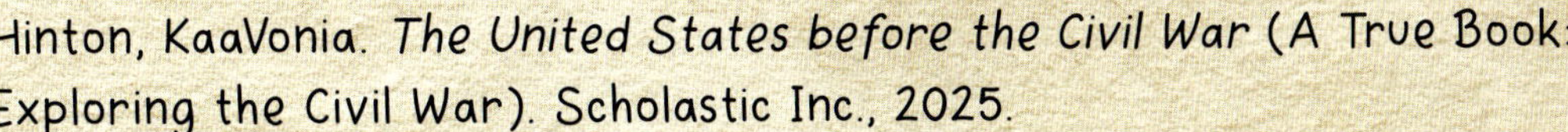

Hinton, KaaVonia. *The United States before the Civil War* (A True Book: Exploring the Civil War). Scholastic Inc., 2025.

McGhee, Jamie. *Reconstruction* (A True Book: Exploring the Civil War). Scholastic Inc., 2025.

Oso, Maisha. *Before the Ships: The Birth of Black Excellence*. Scholastic Inc., 2024.

Rodríguez, Janel. *Civil Rights: Women Who Made a Difference* (Super SHEroes of History). Scholastic Inc., 2023.

Yomtov, Nel. *1955* (Exploring Civil Rights: The Movement). Scholastic Inc., 2022.

Read the other books in this series:

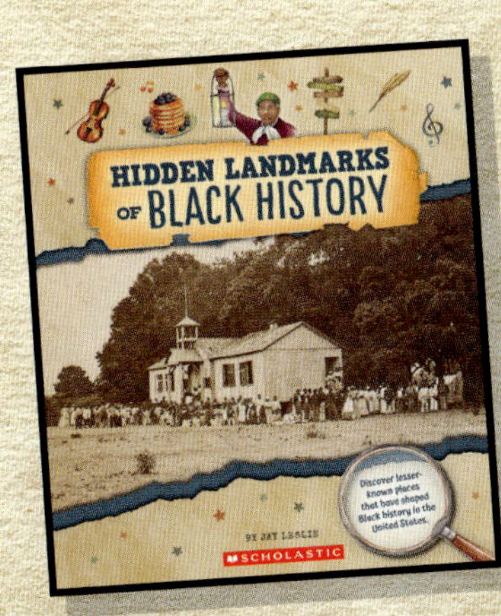

ABOUT THE AUTHOR

KaaVonia Hinton earned a bachelor of science and a master of arts from North Carolina A&T State University and a PhD from the Ohio State University. She is a professor in the Department of Teaching and Learning at Old Dominion University and the author of several nonfiction books for children about US history. Hinton lives in Virginia, where William Tucker, the first person born into slavery in the British colonies in North America, lived.